LIGHT AND DARK

Angela Royston

Heinemann
LIBRARY

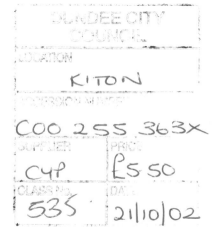

www.heinemann.co.uk/library
Visit our website to find out more information about **Heinemann Library** books.

To order:
☎ Phone 44 (0) 1865 888066
📄 Send a fax to 44 (0) 1865 314091
💻 Visit the Heinemann Bookshop at www.heinemann.co.uk/library to browse our
catalogue and order online.

First published in Great Britain by Heinemann Library, Halley Court, Jordan Hill, Oxford,
OX2 8EJ, a division of Reed Educational & Professional Publishing Ltd. Heinemann is a
registered trademark of Reed Educational & Professional Publishing Ltd.

OXFORD   MELBOURNE   AUCKLAND   JOHANNESBURG   BLANTYRE
GABORONE   IBADAN   PORTSMOUTH NH (USA)   CHICAGO

Designed by bigtop, Bicester, UK
Originated by Ambassador Litho Ltd.
Printed and bound in Hong Kong/China

06 05 04 03 02   06 05 04 03 02
10 9 8 7 6 5 4 3 2   10 9 8 7 6 5 4 3 2 1

ISBN 0 431 13712 9 (hardback)   ISBN 0 431 13718 8 (paperback)

British Library Cataloguing in Publication Data
Royston, Angela
Light and dark. – (My world of science)
1. Light – Juvenile literature
I. Title
535

Acknowledgements
The Publishers would like to thank the following for permission to reproduce photographs:
Corbis: p6, Pablo Corral p26, Ecoscene/Nick Hawkes p25, Kevin Fleming p20, Jim McDonald p13;
Retina: p16; Robert Harding: pp5, 7; Science Photo Library: Bruce Mackie p24; Still Pictures: Jeri
Gleiter p27; Trevor Clifford: pp4, 9, 11, 12, 14, 15, 17, 18, 19, 21, 22, 23, 28, 29; Trip: H Rogers pp8,
10.

Cover photograph reproduced with permission of Robert Harding.

Every effort has been made to contact copyright holders of any material reproduced in this book.
Any omissions will be rectified in subsequent printings if notice is given to the Publisher.

Contents

Any words appearing in the text in bold, **like this**,
are explained in the Glossary.

What is light?

Light allows you to see things. The
boy can see the plant because light
bounces off it and passes into his eyes.

You can see more in bright light than in **dim** light. At night, drivers use lights to see the road and other traffic. How many car **headlights** can you see?

Daylight

It is easy to see during the day.
Daylight comes from the Sun. The Sun's
light is so bright we can see clearly.

Sunlight is so strong it can **damage** your eyes. Never look directly at the Sun. Wear sunglasses in bright sunlight to **protect** your eyes.

Darkness

It is dark at night because the Sun is hidden by the Earth. Some light comes from the Moon and stars. When there is no light, you cannot see anything.

This box is completely closed except for a small hole. If you looked through the hole, it would be too dark inside the box to see anything.

Electric lights

We can make light using **electricity**.
At night we switch on lights so that we
can see. Light bulbs make a bright light.

Televisions and computers use
electricity to light up the screen.
A small green light shows that
the machine is on.

More lights

paraffin lamp

When something burns it makes light.
Candles and paraffin lamps burn
slowly, so they can make light for a
long time.

Fireworks make light too. The light is very bright, but only lasts for a few seconds. Fireworks are easiest to see at night.

Comparing lights

Some lights are brighter than others. The lamp is brighter than the lights on the tree, but **dimmer** than the spotlight. The spotlight is the brightest light.

spotlight

These torches are all shining. The smallest torch is dimmer than the middle torch. Which one is the brightest?

Reflected light

This coat has strips and patches that **gleam** brightly at night. They gleam when light hits them and bounces off. This light is **reflected** light.

Shiny things reflect more light than dull objects. The taps reflect more light than the sponge and towel.

Mirrors

You can see yourself in a mirror.
The mirror **reflects** the light from your
face straight back to you. Mirrors can
also be used to make a light brighter.

The bulb in the torch makes some light, but the shiny surface behind the bulb reflects light too. The reflected light makes the torch brighter.

Transparent objects

Some **materials** are **transparent**. This means that you can see through them. Clear glass is transparent, so you can see the cat through the window.

Plastic can be transparent too. You can see the liquid because most of the light passes through the bottle.

Light-blockers

Some objects let no light pass through them. They are called **opaque**. If you hold a book in front of a light, you will no longer see the light.

This girl is using the door to play 'peek-a-boo' with the child. The child cannot see through the door because the door is opaque.

Light and shade

The Sun gives us most light of all. It bounces off everything around you. When something stops sunlight reaching the ground, it makes a patch of shade.

Clouds make big patches of shade on the ground. You can still see, because there is so much **reflected** light all around you.

Shadows

When an object blocks light, it makes a dark shadow. When the Sun is out, you can see the shadow that your body makes.

These trees are making clear shadows. The shadows are in front of the trees. Where do you think the Sun is – in front or behind?

Shadow shapes

Light always travels in straight lines.
The light is blocked where the vase is.
This means that the shadow is the
same shape as the vase.

You can use your hands to make interesting shadows. What does this shadow look like? If you wave your hand, your shadow seems to say 'goodbye'!

Glossary

damage hurt or injure

dim half-dark

electricity power or force that can make something work

gleam shine

headlight large light at the front of a car, bus, lorry or other vehicle

material what something is made of

opaque something which lets no light through it

protect look after

reflect bounce back light

transparent something clear which you can see through

Answers

Page 5 – What is light?
There are eight car headlights in the photo.

Page 15 – Comparing lights
The biggest torch, the one on the left, is the brightest.

Page 27 – Shadows
The Sun is behind the trees.

Page 29 – Shadow shapes
The shadow looks like a bird.

Index